The Artner

Reader's Guide
to American History

A Memoria Press Study Guide

by Kathy Artner

Artner Reader's Guide To American History

American History Reading Guide for Grades 3-8

An Extensive List of the Great Writers of Children's History Books

Basic Fact Sheets and Optional Activites for Each Historical Period

How to Find Books so Exciting and Memorable That Your Children Will Read Them Over and Over

A Not to be Missed History Series for Children by Some of America's Greatest Writers

Poems and Songs That "Capture" Eras in American History

How to Find Out-of-Print Books at Bargain Basement Prices

How to Create a Library of Classical History Books to Hand Down in Your Family

DOCERE. DELECTARE. MOVERE.

Other Study Guides by Memoria Press:
Henle Latin Study Guide and Lesson Plan for Units I & II
Classical Studies Guide for
- •D'Aulaires' Greek Myths
- •Famous Men of Rome
- •The Golden Children's Bible

Other Books From Memoria Press:
Latina Christiana: An Introduction to Christian Latin
Lingua Angelica: Latin Reading Program
Traditional Logic: An Introduction to Formal Logic

Artner Reader's Guide to American History
© 2000 by Memoria Press LLC

ISBN 1-930953-16-X

4103 Bishop Lane, Louisville, KY 40218
www.memoriapress.com

TABLE OF CONTENTS

Preface

We believe that the best way to teach your child history is by having him read lots of well-written stories about the men and women who made history. Textbooks alone are much less effective—and certainly less interesting. In fact, we believe that history textbooks are unnecessary during the elementary years, except as a guide for parents. Though generally unable to analyze trends or identify complex causal relationships, a child at this level *can* accumulate a wealth of stories and mental images about the people (famous or forgotten) who made our country great.

Adults often complain that their own experience with the study of history amounted to little more than rote memorization of the dates of unrelated events. History does not have to be this hard or tedious. If your child learns about the major conflicts in our country's history and a *few* well-chosen dates, the rest will fall logically into place. A child who has read stories about the lives of Ben Franklin and Thomas Edison is hardly likely to think the two lived at the same time, or place the invention of the light bulb before the American Revolution.

While your child doesn't need to memorize a lengthy list of dates and events, he does need to have a general understanding of each historical period. This can be accomplished very simply—a brief explanation coupled with the use of a timeline and map. Your child will not only read more effectively, but will be more interested in what he reads.

Think of it as building a house. By briefly discussing the major events of a period with your child, you are pouring the foundation and framing the house. With that work done, the stories your child reads will build on that foundation, and finish the house. Conversely, if your child does not have that basic knowledge, he will not have the context necessary to fully understand what he is reading.

Children learn history best by reading accurate and well-written historical narratives, especially those that emphasize heroism and character. While this is not a particularly revolutionary view of the subject, we do think it often goes unheeded, which is why we emphasize it. More importantly, this view determines the resources we have chosen to include in this guide.

Fiction vs. Nonfiction

Historical fiction is an excellent complement to real history. But while there is much to be said for historical fiction, the emphasis when studying history should logically be on actual histories. A talented author of good historical fiction captures the reader by embellishing real history with exciting fictional characters and events—that is why we have included much of it in this guide. However, though historical novels can help young readers visualize a historical period, they can't treat it systematically. That's the role of history texts.

Fortunately, when educating children about history, we are not forced to choose between interesting and enjoyable historical fiction on the one hand, and dull, ponderous histories on the other. As you will see, the best children's histories have the same characteristics as the best historical fiction: exciting characters, compelling stories, and interesting dialogue.

What is Wrong with Today's History Books?

After looking at our reading lists, the first question the teacher might have is "why are so many of the books you've chosen out of print?" While there are notable exceptions, the sad fact is that most of the history books written for children today are vastly inferior to the children's books that were written in the 1940's and 1950's. Of course, every year, there are some excellent children's books published, but the educational value of all too many new books is marginal at best.

Why is that the case? Unfortunately, the majority of new history books, particularly those for intermediate readers, emphasize exquisite photographs and amazing graphics over the actual text itself. Even many new biographies seem written to entertain in short bursts rather than thoroughly tell a story. Children at this level need to move away from a reliance on picture-intensive books. If anything, children in this visually dominated society of computers and television need to read more stories, not stare at more images. Most videos and picture books can only convey a portion of what a book can, and sometimes a very misleading portion at that.

As an example of the "dumbing-down" of children's history books, consider the fact that a Landmark book written in the 1950's for grades four and up averaged around 175 pages. A Lerner biography written today for grades 3-6 averages 80-90 pages. Perhaps the writers and publishers fear that there is no more market for lengthier children's books. Our view is that this is precisely the time when children need to develop the reading habits that they will carry through life. They need to read books that are long enough to give them both the factual information they require, as well as the flavor of what life was like

Ironically, in the attempt to make history more accessible by decreasing text, modern publishers have dramatically increased the amount of misinformation. You've probably read news accounts about studies chronicling the grotesque errors riddling many elementary and secondary textbooks. Unfortunately, you simply can no longer assume that a history book has the facts right. Somehow, in the process of reducing the amount of text, we have been subjected to a dismaying
increase in the amount of historical inaccuracy.

Then there is the matter of political bias. Many of today's history texts have replaced a generally positive portrayal of our nation's history with an increas-ingly negative one. While we do not want to ignore the undeniably tragic and shameful chapters of American history, <u>at this age</u> it is important to emphasize the heroic nature of our country's leaders. We believe that one goal of history at this level should be to nurture a respectful attitude toward the admittedly imperfect institutions our nation has created. As your children grow older, there will be plenty of time to deal more fully with all of America's faults.

Great History by Great Writers

We must not make the mistake of painting all new books with the same brush. Some recently published history series are historically accurate. Yet they often seem to have been churned out by competent writers with no true expertise or abiding interest in what they're writing about. If you want to create a love of history among all readers, you need books written by good writers who know their subject matter. A child who is naturally enthusiastic about the Civil War, for example, will read and enjoy almost any book on Gettysburg, regardless of the writing style. However, reluctant readers of history need a well-written book to truly engage their interest.

Don't mistake glitzy graphics or fun facts for good writing. Although these can definitely add interest to a book, such gimmicks are no substitute for a compelling narrative. Some parents would argue, "Well, it's the only thing I can get my child to read on the subject and something is better than nothing." This is simply wrong. Sometimes nothing is preferable to something— especially if the something being offered trivializes the subject. A child should learn to expect well-written books whether the topic is fantasy, history or science.

In fact, the benefits of reading well-written history go beyond the discipline of history itself. A child's writing is dramatically affected by what he reads. If he reads dull prose, he will write dull prose. Worse, he may not write at all. Conversely, if he reads well-written prose, he is more likely to write well-written prose. In short, good reading fosters good writing.

Finally, if a child is introduced to history through engaging, exciting books, he will quickly learn to love reading. By reading the kinds of books we have included in this guide, your child will not only enjoy history, but enjoy books, a goal of every parent. And let's face it, a love of books is the key to a lifelong

Some Notable Series and Authors
Despite the disappointing quality of many recently published books, good history books for young people are not hard to find if you know what to look for. As you will discover by reading our appendix at the back of this guide, there are several ways to obtain these books that do not require a homeschooling mother to spend all her spare time book-hunting. A few of the series and notable authors we have chosen to include are highlighted below.

Landmark Books
The Landmark Books are a series of non-fiction books published by Random House in the fifties and early sixties. Simply put, the Landmark series is the best collection of children's histories ever written. As a jacket blurb on an old edition stated, "The reasons [for the series' popularity] are obvious: good writers and important and appealing subjects from America's past."

Writers in the Landmark series include such notable children's authors as **Ralph Moody** (author of the *Little Britches* series), **Jim Kjelgaard** (*Big Red*), **James Daugherty** (Caldecott winner *Daniel Boone*), **Armstrong Sperry** (*Call It Courage*) and **Dorothy Canfield Fisher** (author of the classic *Understood Betsy*). **Sterling North** (author of *Rascal*), was another Landmark author. Sterling North was also editor of a series of non-fiction books for young people entitled North Star, some of which we've included on our list. The other writers in the series, though less well known, are generally first-rate.

The series editors were clever enough to match authors with their fields of interest. For example, **Ralph Moody** grew up out West at the turn of the century, as he chronicled in the *Little Britches* series. His Landmark titles include *Kit Carson and the Wild Frontier* and *Geronimo: Wolf of the Warpath*. He also wrote a book entitled *Wells Fargo* for another series, which is included on our list. **Armstrong Sperry's** books dovetail with his lifelong interest in the sea—*The Voyages of Christopher Columbus*, and *John Paul Jones, Fighting Sailor.*

Children's authors weren't the only ones who wrote Landmarks. **C.S. Forester**, known for the *Horatio Hornblower* series and *The African Queen*, wrote a book on the Barbary Pirates which our son loved. **Shirley Jackson**, author of *The Lottery*, wrote a book titled *The Witchcraft of Salem Village* that is now back in print. **Ted Lawson** (*Thirty Seconds Over Tokyo*) and **Richard Tregaskis** (*Guadalcanal Diary*) wrote versions of these two books for the Landmark series. **Robert Penn Warren**, author of the Pulitzer prize winning *All the King's Men*, wrote *Remember the Alamo* for Landmark.

Some of the authors mentioned above wrote notable non-fiction for children outside the Landmark series. We've included many of those we have come across. We're sure there are others still to be found.

Childhood of Famous Americans Series
The Childhood of Famous Americans series was originally published in the 1960s. All are back in print. As the series' title indicates, the books deal mainly with the childhood and only briefly discuss, if at all, the adult accomplishments of the famous men and women profiled. While not up to the level of a Landmark, they are an excellent series for a young reader just beginning chapter books.

SPECIFIC AUTHORS
Ronald Syme
Mr. Syme definitely has an abiding interest in the famous explorers he writes about. He went to sea at 18, traveling to many parts of the world writing short stories and feature articles. In 1934, he became a full-time journalist until war broke out. For a while, he served in the British Merchant Service as a ship's gunner. Eventually, he settled in Rarotonga in the Cook Islands in the South Pacific. According to the author sketch at the back of one of his books, he can check almost any historical fact he needs for his writing by consulting his own personal library. In most of his books, Mr. Syme writes in a style particularly appropriate for the younger reader. Though currently out of print, his books are available in most library systems and many used bookstores.

The D'Aulaires
Little needs to be said about our inclusion of the D'Auliare biographies. They have become classics in their own right and can be read profitably at any age.

Albert Marrin
As we said earlier, not all the good children's history books are 30 or 40 years old. In fact, one of our favorite writers is still writing today. Albert Marrin, in addition to teaching history at the college level, also writes excellent history books for children. Besides books on U.S. Grant and Robert E. Lee, Marrin has written perhaps the best children's treatment of the French and Indian Wars. Since Marrin's books are beyond the reading level of most third graders, I have included them in a special *Advanced Reader/ Read Aloud* section. They would make a fabulous read-aloud, but be forewarned that some of the topics concern violent periods in our history and parts may not be suitable for younger children.

Other Excellent Writers
We've included several other notable children's authors on our lists. They include **Esther Forbes** (*Johnny Tremain),* **Clyde Robert Bulla** (an excellent author of beginning chapter books), **Holling Clancy Hollings** (*Paddle-to-the-Sea)* and **Jean Lee Latham** (*Carry On, Mr. Bowditch).* **Colonel Red Reeder** wrote a series of military history books for young people, including the Landmark *The West Point Story.* Colonel Reeder, a graduate of West Point, was a decorated veteran of several wars.

The Medveds' "1960 Rule" and Current Authors
In Michael and Diane Medved's excellent *Saving Childhood: Protecting Our Children from the National Assault on Innocence*, they discuss a rule they instituted for their three children when they go to the library: the kids must have their parents look at any book published after 1960 before checking it out. While we readily agree that many history books written today often suffer from political correctness, we do not believe that every book written before 1960 is necessarily worthwhile or that every book written after 1960 should be avoided.

Russell Freedman, a contemporary author, has written several excellent books on the American West and one photobiography on Lincoln that earned a Newbery Award. We have included two of his books on our list. **Jean Fritz** is another excellent working writer who has written a massive number of non-fiction titles. While we feel that some of her books for younger readers border on the trivial, her book on the writing of the Constitution is extremely well-researched and even manages to explain the differing philosophies of the Federalists and Jeffersonians in a way that would be understandable to her readers. Her biographies for upper elementary readers on Sam Houston, Stonewall Jackson and Teddy Roosevelt are also well-done.

Primary Sources
Finally, we have tried to include some primary sources that can be understood by a 3rd -5th grader. *The Log of Christopher Columbus, Homes in the Wilderness, Pilgrim Voices, The Boys' War and Yankee Doodle Boy, The Story of my Life* (Helen Keller) and *The Spirit of St. Louis* (Charles Lindbergh) are examples of these.

This list is certainly not meant to be comprehensive. We're sure you'll find some forgotten gems in your own searches. Our goal was simply to provide a *manageable* list of *quality* books organized in such a way that your trip to the library will be as painless and successful as possible.

While the local public library is an excellent resource for homeschooling parents, having a library at home is an indispensable benefit for any family that values education. Many of these books are treasures that you will want every one of your children to read. A guide to finding these out-of-print treasures is in the Appendix.

Reading Plan

For the most part, we have followed the editors of the acclaimed Landmark Book series in dividing American History into eight major units. We have diverged from their timeline in two ways: we combined two pre-Civil War themes, and split the post-World War One era into two sections.

Reading levels—like grade levels in school—are very arbitrary. For example, we've seen *Across Five Aprils* listed as 7th and up, and 5th and up. We remember reading it in the 4th or 5th grade. Who's right? You are the best judge when picking up a book as to whether your childen can read it. And let's face it, if it's something they're keenly interested in, they can probably read a book above their actual reading level and enjoy it.

We have designed this Teacher's Guide to give you maximum flexibility. Depending on your child's independent reading level, you can begin Unit 1 as early as third grade. We feel you should complete Unit 8 by the end of the eighth grade. Within those broad guidelines, you are free to move through the units at your own pace.

HOW TO USE THE RESOURCE GUIDE

Each Unit in the Resource Guide consists of three sections:

Basic Facts Sheet
1. Chronological List of Important Events with Dates
2. People, Places and Events to Read About
3. Inventions and Innovations
4. Important Documents and Policies
5. Famous Expressions
6. Page References to *Everything You Need to Know About American History Homework*

Study Helps
7. Study Topics from E. D. Hirsch, Jr.
8. Optional Activities

Reading Lists
9. Reading Lists
10. Poetry, Prose and Songs

Basic Facts Sheet

Using the **Basic Facts Sheet** and *Everything You Need to Know About American History Homework,* briefly discuss with your child the historical period you have chosen for study. Be forewarned that this text, like all contemporary history books, occasionally suffers from political correctness but does provide an accurate reference for parents. Feel free to supplement with any textbooks, encyclopedias or other books you have on hand.

Study Helps

If you want to spend more time than the quick overview suggested above, we recommend topics from E.D. Hirsch's *Core Knowledge* series. These books are named for the various grades: *What Your 3rd Grader Needs to Know, What Your 4th Grader Needs to Know,* etc. You may remember that Hirsch's surprise bestseller *Cultural Literacy: What Every American Needs to Know,* was one of the first mainstream books which pointed out the inadequacy of what is being taught in so many of our schools. We have found the history sections of the Hirsch books to be especially well-written and helpful. Most libraries have copies of these books, so you may check them out or read them while you are there. Most of the articles are quite short, about a page. The material for a particular period could easily be covered in a week.

Additional independent work is included under "Optional Activities," some of which are keyed to *Everything You Need to Know About American History Homework.*

Reading Lists

For the first three units, we've included two levels of reading lists. The first level contains some simple biographies for students who have just begun to read chapter books. Once your children can read longer books comfortably, move them to the second level or **main list.**

The **Main List** is divided into four sections: ***in-print and easily found, out-of-print Landmarks, other out-of-print treasures*** and ***advanced readers***. The ***advanced reader*** section includes titles we feel are extremely noteworthy but may be beyond your child's reading level. You are the ultimate judge. An option may be to read the book aloud. A well-written non-fiction book can be as engaging as the best in fiction.

As a bonus, we have included a brief list of ***historical fiction,*** which is often more easily found than non-fiction titles. Note: most historical fiction needs some background explanation, especially if your children are unfamiliar with the setting of the story.

Reading List Terms.
CFA—Childhood of Famous Americans series
North Star—a series of non-fiction books edited by Sterling North
Newbery and *Newbery Honor*— books that received this distinguished award
*—denotes a family favorite
Books that contain difficult or disturbing material have also been noted.

Poetry, Prose and Song
These are poems, songs or prose selections related to the period that you can read (or sing) and discuss with your child. You may also choose to assign one or two for memorization. All can easily be found in the library or on the web. Two excellent sources are: *The Harp and Laurel Wreath*, edited by Laura Berquist and *The American Reader: Words That Moved a Nation*, edited by Diane Ravitch. The Hirsch books also include some of the selections in the "Stories and Speeches" or "Poetry" sections.

STEP BY STEP SCHEDULE FOR TEACHING EACH UNIT

1. **Introduce the historical period.** Refer to the **Basic Facts Sheet** and supplement with the maps, charts and other helps in *Everything You Need to Know About American History Homework.* If you want a more comprehensive introduction, read aloud the suggested sections in the Hirsch books (which we highly recommend). Spend as much time here as you desire. By the third grade, most children have some idea about early American history so this preparation time need not be too elaborate

2. **Post a copy of the Basic Facts Sheet on your school wall** so you can refer to it throughout the year. Have your child read the names on the **Basic Facts Sheet** periodically throughout the year until he can do so with ease. Occasionally have your child identify as many people, places and events as he can from the list. Copybook exercises are valuable for younger students. Copybook exercises involve copying the names, places and events on the **Basic Facts Sheet** in a permanent "copybook" of their best writing. When they do copybook work, students practice penmanship and spelling as they become familiar with the people, places and events of American history.

3. **Assign the dates.** Important dates in history are listed at the top of each **Basic Facts Sheet**. These should be committed to memory and reviewed throughout the year and in subsequent years as more dates are added.

4. **Select books** to read from the list provided. When a book has been selected, you may want to review the particular background facts to make your child's reading more profitable. An eager student might be motivated to mark off as many boxes on his book list as possible. Discuss books with your child during the year and refer to the **Basic Facts Sheet** or other resources when needed.

5. **Occasionally select a book from the historical fiction or advanced reader list** for a family read-aloud. A great way to get Dad involved!

6. **Optional activities** can be done at your discretion. They should not take away from reading time since that is the most valuable activity in the course.

7. **Poetry, Prose and Songs** can be assigned periodically. For example, if there is a speech that you would like your child to learn, you may introduce it at this time, perhaps during the weekly poetry session. Later, the speech could be written down in the child's copybook.

History Units

Exploration and Settlement
(c.1000-1607)

**Dates
and Events
to Remember**

c.1000 ------- Vikings sail to "Vinland"
1492 --------- First voyage of Columbus
1521 --------- Cortes conquers the Aztecs
French explore St. Lawrence and Mississippi Rivers
Dutch explore New York
English explore Atlantic coast
Spanish Explore Florida & California

**People
Places and Topics
to Read About**

Christopher Columbus   Captain James Cook
Ferdinand Magellan   John Cabot
Hernando Cortes   Verrazano
The Vikings   Pizarro
Leif Erikson   Ponce de Leon
Jacques Cartier   Coronado
Samuel de Champlain   De Soto
Henry Hudson   Vasco de Gama
Balboa   Francis Drake

Everything You Need to Know About American History Homework:
A Desk Reference for Students and Parents

"European Explorers Find a New World"   Pages 6-8

UNIT 1: STUDY HELPS

- Early Visitors to North America—The Vikings
- Finding—and Taking—a "New World"
- Spanish Explorers of North America
- Spanish Settlements in the New World
- In Search of the Northwest Passage
- New France
- The Voyages of Henry Hudson
- The Land Shapes the Ways People Live
- Location of Indian tribes
- Explanation of the reasons for European exploration

Study Topics from E. D. Hirsch's *What Your 3rd Grader Needs to Know*

Optional Activities
(Page numbers are keyed to *Everything You Need to Know About American History Homework*)

- List and memorize the five reasons for European exploration (p. 6)
- Trace the journeys of Columbus on a map of the Caribbean
- Pretend that you are one of the explorers you are reading about. Write a letter back to your parents describing your journey

UNIT I: READING LISTS

Level 1 Reading out-of-print

- ☑ *Amerigo Vespucci: Scientist and Sailor*, Ronald Syme — *we own*
- ☐ *Balboa, Finder of the Pacific*, Ronald Syme
- ☐ *Captain Cook, Pacific Explorer*, Ronald Syme
- ☐ *Cartier, Finder of the St. Lawrence*, Ronald Syme — *Library*
- ☐ *Champlain of the St. Lawrence*, Ronald Syme
- ☐ *Columbus, Finder of the New World*, Ronald Syme
- ☐ *Cortes of Mexico*, Ronald Syme
- ☐ *De Soto, Finder of the Mississippi*, Ronald Syme
- ☐ *First Man to Cross America* (Cabeza de Vaca), Ronald Syme
- ☐ *Francisco Coronado and the Seven Cities of Gold*, Ronald Syme
- ☐ *Francis Drake, Sailor of the Unknown Seas*, Ronald Syme
- ☐ *Francisco Pizarro, Finder of Peru*, Ronald Syme
- ☐ *Henry Hudson*, Ronald Syme — *library we own*
- ☐ *John Cabot and his Son Sebastian*, Ronald Syme
- ☐ *LaSalle of the Mississippi*, Ronald Syme
- ☑ *Magellan, First Around the World*, Ronald Syme — *we own*
- ☐ *The Man Who Discovered the Amazon*, Ronald Syme
- ☐ *Vasco de Gama, Sailor Toward the Sunrise*, Ronald Syme
- ☐ *Verrazano, Explorer of the Atlantic Coast*, Ronald Syme
- ☐ *Walter Raleigh*, Ronald Syme — *half.com*

Level 2 Reading: In-Print or Easily Found

- ☐ *The Vikings*, Elizabeth Janeway (Landmark) — *library*
- ☐ *The Log of Christopher Columbus* (abridged) — *library*
- ☑ *Brendan the Navigator*, Jean Fritz — *library read*
- ☐ *Cartier Sails the St. Lawrence*, Esther Averill — *half.com*

Landmarks (out-of-print)

Bought from Amazon

- ☐ *The Voyages of Christopher Columbus*, Armstrong Sperry
- ☐ *Captain Cook Explores the South Seas*, Armstrong Sperry
- ☐ *The Hudson's Bay Company*, Richard Morenus
- ☐ *Balboa: Swordsman and Conquistador*, Felix Riesenberg, Jr.
- ☐ *Ferdinand Magellan: Master Mariner*, Seymour Gates Pond
- ☐ *Captain Cortes Conquers Mexico*, William Johnson
- ☐ *Walter Raleigh, Man of Two Worlds*, Henrietta Buckmaster
- ☐ *The Voyages of Henry Hudson*, Eugene Rachlis

UNIT 1: READING LISTS

□ *Admiral Christopher Columbus*, Clara Ingram Judson

Other Out-of-Print Treasures

□ *The Sea King: Sir Francis Drake and his Times*, Albert Marrin *library*
□ *Aztecs and Spaniards: Cortes and the Conquest of Mexico*, Albert Marrin *library*
□ *Inca and Spaniard: Pizarro and the Conquest of Peru*, Albert Marrin *half, or*
□ *Empires Lost and Won: The Spanish Heritage in the Southwest*, Albert
    Marrin (describes events up through the Alamo and the Mexican War) *library*

Advanced Readers or Read-Aloud

☑ **The Story of Rolf and the Viking Bow*, Allen French *library*
□ *Door to the North*, Elizabeth Coatsworth

Historical Fiction

"Christopher Columbus," Stephen Vincent Benet
"Columbus," Joaquin Miller
"Hernando de Soto," Rosemary and Stephen Vincent Benet

Poetry, Prose and Songs

* Family favorite

The Colonial Period (1607-1775)

**Dates
and Events
to Remember**

1607 --------- Jamestown founded
1620 --------- Mayflower lands
1754-1763 --- French and Indian Wars
Indians teach colonists how to raise tobacco
Franciscan missions established in California

**People
Places and Topics to
Read About**

Pilgrims
Puritans
Plymouth Colony
Jamestown
Pocahontas
Captain John Smith
Squanto
Fr. Junipero Serra
Kateri Tekakwitha
Pere Marquette
St. Isaac Jogues
Ben Franklin
Daniel Boone
Iroquois Confederacy
Lord Baltimore
Roger Williams
William Penn
Massachusetts Bay Colony

**Important
Documents
to Research**

Mayflower Compact

Everything You Need to Know About American History Homework:
A Desk Reference for Students and Parents

"Colonization of the Americas"
"North America Before 1775"

Pages 9-19

UNIT 2: STUDY HELPS

- The First Americans
- East of the Mississippi
- Familiar Names
- The Lost Colony of Roanoke
- Jamestown Colony: Hard Beginnings
- Tobacco: A "Cash Crop"
- The Pilgrims at Plymouth
- Massachusetts Bay: The Puritans
- More Colonies
- Farther South
- Hard Labor
- Songhai
- Benin
- *Sarah Sees a "Walking"
- *How the "Walk" Began
- *What Sarah Saw
- *A Day with Little Thunder
- *Everyone Works
- *At the Games
- *Trouble Ahead
- *Shall We Go to War?

* Optional selections (but well worth it!)

Study Topics from E. D. Hirsch's *What Your 3rd Grader Needs to Know*

Optional Activities
(Page numbers are keyed to *Everything You Need to Know About American History Homework*)

- List and memorize the 13 colonies (pp. 16-17)
- Describe the differences between the colonies in different regions (p. 9, 11)
- Trace your own map of the 13 colonies (see map, p. 9)
- Pretend you are a young person living in one of the colonies. Write a description of a day in your life (p. 11)
- Suppose that you were responsible for outfitting Marquette and Joliet's expedition: what kind of supplies would you take?

UNIT 2: READING LISTS

Level 1 Reading

☐ *Pocahontas*, Ingri and Edgar Parin D'Aulaire *library*
☐ *Squanto: First Friend of the Pilgrims*, Clyde Robert Bulla
☐ *Pocahontas and the Strangers*, Clyde Robert Bulla
☐ *Stranded at Plymouth Plantation*, Gary Bowen
☐ *Ben Franklin*, Ingri and Edgar Parin D'Aulaire
☐ *Abigail Adams: Girl of Colonial Days*, Wagoner (CFA)
☐ *Ben Franklin: Young Printer*, Stevenson (CFA)
☐ *Daniel Boone: Young Tracker*, Stevenson (CFA)
☐ *Frontenac of New France*, Ronald Syme
☐ *John Smith of Virginia*, Ronald Syme
☐ *Marquette and Joliet: Voyagers on the Mississippi*, Ronald Syme *library*
☐ *William Penn, Founder of Pennsylvania*, Ronald Syme

Level 2 Reading: In-Print or Easily Found

☐ *The Landing of the Pilgrims*, James Daugherty (Landmark)
☐ *Ben Franklin of Old Philadelphia*, Margaret Cousins (Landmark)
☐ *Pilgrim Voices*, Edited by Connie and Peter Roop
☐ *Homes in the Wilderness: A Pilgrim's Journal of Plymouth Plantation in 1620*, William Bradford
☐ *Father Marquette and the Great Rivers*, August Derleth
☐ *The Witchcraft of Salem Village*, Shirley Jackson (Landmark)
☐ *Kateri Takekwitha: Mohawk Maid*, Evelyn Brown
☐ *The Story of Junipero Serra, Brave Adventurer*, Florence Meiman White
☐ *Saint Isaac and the Indians*, Milton Lomask
☐ *Daniel Boone: His Own Story*, Daniel Boone
☐ *Daniel Boone*, James Daugherty, Newbery

Landmarks (out-of-print)

☐ *The Explorations of Pere Marquette*, Jim Kjelgaard
☐ *William Penn: Quaker Statesman*, Hildegarde Dolson
☐ *George Washington: Frontier Colonel*, Sterling North
☐ *Peter Stuyvesant of Old New York*, Anna and Russel Crouse
☐ *Pocahontas and Captain John Smith*, Marie Lawson
☐ *Daniel Boone*, John Mason Brown *we own*
☐ *The Mississippi Bubble*, Thomas B. Costain
☐ *Rogers' Rangers and the French and Indian War*, Bradford Smith
☐ *Evangeline and the Acadians*, Robert Tallant
☐ *The Story of the Thirteen Colonies*, Clifford Alderman
☐ *Famous Pirates of the New World*, A. B. C. Whipple

UNIT 2: READING LISTS

☐ *Ticonderoga: The Story of a Fort*, Bruce Lancaster (North Star)
☐ *Captured by the Mohawks*, Sterling North (North Star)
☐ *America's Ethan Allen*, Stewart Holbrook
☐ *Flames Over New England*, Olga Hall-Quest

Other Out-of-Print Treasures

☐ *Struggle for a Continent: The French and Indian Wars, 1690-1760, Albert Marrin

Advanced Readers or Read-Aloud

Historical Fiction

☐ *The Courage of Sarah Noble*, Alice Dalgliesh, Newbery Honor

Level 1

Level 2

☐ **Madeleine Takes Command*, Ethel Brill
☑ **The Matchlock Gun*, Walter Edmonds, Newbery *we our*
☐ **The Sign of the Beaver*, Elizabeth George Speare, Newbery Honor *we our*
☐ *Amos Fortune, Free Man*, Elizabeth Yates, Newbery *we our*
☐ *Benjamin West and his Cat Grimalkin*, Marguerite Henry
☐ *Justin Morgan Had a Horse,* Marguerite Henry, Newbery Honor
☐ *The Tavern at the Ferry*, Edwin Tunis
☐ *Indian Captive*, Lois Lenski, Newbery Honor
☑ *The Witch of Blackbird Pond*, Elizabeth Speare, Newbery (older reader) *library, we our*
☑ *Calico Captive*, Elizabeth Speare (older reader)
☐ *Sword of the Wilderness*, Elizabeth Coatsworth
☐ *Drummer Boy for Montcalm*, Wilma Pitchford Hays
☐ *Daniel Boone's Echo*, William O. Steele (tall tales)
☑ *Calico Bush*, Rachel Field, Newbery Honor (older reader) *we our*

Poetry, Prose and Songs

Songs
"Yankee Doodle"

Poems
"Pocahontas," William Makepeace Thackeray
"Pocahontas," Rosemary Benet

The War of Independence and the New Government (1775-1789)

Dates and Events to Remember

The Boston Tea Party
Paul Revere's Ride/Lexington and Concord
1776 --------- Declaration of Independence
Winter at Valley Forge
1783 --------- Treaty of Paris ends the War
1789 --------- Washington becomes first president

People Places and Topics to Read About

Ben Franklin
George Washington
Thomas Jefferson
Patrick Henry
Thomas Paine
John Adams
Crossing the Delaware
Betsy Ross
Paul Revere
John Paul Jones
Ethan Allen
Saratoga
Valley Forge
Molly Pitcher

Yorktown
Marquis de Lafayette
Benedict Arnold
Lord Cornwallis
Lexington and Concord
Crispus Attucks
James Madison
Abigail Adams
Nathan Hale
The minutemen
Poor Richard's Almanack
The Liberty Bell
Bunker Hill

Important Documents to Research

Declaration of Independence
Constitution
Bill of Rights
Articles of Confederation

Famous Phrases

The shot heard 'round the world
Give me liberty or give me death
I have not yet begun to fight

The times that try men's souls
Taxation without representation
Our lives, our fortunes, our sacred honor

Everything You Need to Know About American History Homework:
A Desk Reference for Students and Parents

"The American Revolution"
"The Birth of New Nation"
Appendix B

Pages 20-33
Pages 113-123

UNIT 3: STUDY HELPS

Study Topics from E. D. Hirsch's *What Your 3rd Grader Needs to Know*

Study Topics from E. D. Hirsch's *What Your 4th Grader Needs to Know*

Optional Activities
(Page numbers are keyed to *Everything You Need to Know About American History Homework*)

- Draw a diagram illustrating the system of checks and balances (p. 114)
- Draw a diagram illustrating the three branches of government (p. 115)
- List and memorize key people in the new nation and briefly describe each (p. 33)
- Create a map of the Boston area, and trace the route taken by Paul Revere
- Draw a map showing how the British planned to split the colonies in two, before being stopped at Saratoga
- Suppose you owned a newspaper during the Revolutionary War - write a news story explaining the new Declaration of Independence

UNIT 3: READING LISTS

**Level 1
Reading:
In-Print**

- [ ] *George Washington*, Ingri and Edgar Parin D'Aulaire *library*
- [ ] *Patrick Henry: Voice of American Revolution*, Louis Sabin
- [ ] *Betsy Ross: Designer of our Flag*, Weil (CFA)
- [ ] *Crispus Attucks: Black Leader of Colonial Patriots*, Millender (CFA)
- [ ] *George Washington: Young Leader*, Stevenson (CFA)
- [ ] *Martha Washington: America's First Lady*, Wagoner (CFA)
- [ ] *Molly Pitcher: Young Patriot*, Stevenson (CFA)
- [ ] *Paul Revere: Boston Patriot*, Stevenson (CFA)
- [ ] *Tom Jefferson: Third President of the US*, Monsell (CFA)
- [ ] *Captain John Paul Jones: America's Fighting Seaman*, Ronald Syme
- [ ] *Benedict Arnold: Traitor of the Revolution*, Ronald Syme

**Level 2
Reading:
In-Print
or Easily Found**

- [ ] *The American Revolution*, Bruce Bliven, Jr. (Landmark)
- [ ] *Our Independence and the Constitution*, Dorothy Canfield Fisher (Landmark)
- [ ] *Ben Franklin of Old Philadelphia*, Margaret Cousins (Landmark)
- [ ] *Shhh! We're Writing the Constitution*, Jean Fritz *we own*
- [ ] *If You Were There When They Signed the Constitution*, Elizabeth Levy
- [ ] *George Washington: The Man Who Would Not Be King*, Stephen Krensky

**Level 2
Reading:
Landmarks
(out-of-print)**

- [ ] *Paul Revere and the Minute Men*, Dorothy Canfield Fisher *(we own)*
- [ ] *The Winter at Valley Forge*, Van Wyck Mason
- [ ] *Thomas Jefferson, Father of Democracy*, Vincent Sheean
- [ ] *John Paul Jones, Fighting Sailor*, Armstrong Sperry
- [ ] *Ethan Allen and the Green Mountain Boys*, Slater Brown
- [ ] **The Swamp Fox of the Revolution,* Stewart H. Holbrook
- [ ] *Betsy Ross and the Flag*, Jane Mayer

**Other
Out-of-Print
Treasures**

- [ ] *The Story of the Revolutionary War*, Colonel Red Reeder
- [ ] *George Washington: Leader of the People*, Clara Ingram Judson
- [ ] *Thomas Jefferson: Champion of the People*, Clara Ingram Judson
- [ ] *Benjamin Franklin*, Clara Ingram Judson
- [ ] *America's Paul Revere*, Esther Forbes

**Advanced
Reader
or Read-Aloud**

- [ ] **The War for Independence: The Story of the American Revolution*, Albert Marrin
- [ ] *The Great Little Madison*, Jean Fritz *we own*
- [ ] *Traitor: The Case of Benedict Arnold*, Jean Fritz

UNIT 3: READING LISTS

Historical Fiction

☐ *Ben and Me*, Robert Lawson
☐ *Mr. Revere and I*, Robert Lawson
☐ *Early Thunder*, Jean Fritz
☐ *Johnny Tremain*, Esther Forbes, (Newbery) *we own*
☐ *Drums*, James Boyd
☐ *Guns for General Washington*, Seymour Reit
☐ *The Cabin Faced West*, Jean Fritz *we own*
☐ *Toliver's Secret*, Esther Wood Brady
☐ *The Reb and the Redcoats*, Constance Savery
☐ *The Year of the Bloody Sevens*, William O. Steele
☐ *Special Picture Book: Paul Revere's Ride—Illustrated by Ted Rand* *we own*
☐ *John Paul Jones, Soldier of the Sea*, Donald E. Worcester

Poetry and Prose

Prose

"The Declaration of Independence"
"The Bill of Rights"
Preamble to "The Constitution"
"The War Inevitable", March 1775, Patrick Henry
"Washington's Address to His Troops"
"Washington on His Appointment as Commander-in-Chief"

Poetry

"America for Me". Henry Van Dyke
"The Flag Goes By", Henry Holcomb Bennett
"George Washington", Stephen Vincent Benet
"Benjamin Franklin", Stephen Vincent Benet
"John Paul Jones", Stephen Vincent Benet
"Paul Revere's Ride", Henry Wadsworth Longfellow
"Concord Hymn", Ralph Waldo Emerson
"Hiawatha's Childhood" from "Song of Hiawatha", Henry Wadsworth Longfellow

* family favorites

National Development and Westward Expansion (1790-1877)

Dates and Events to Remember

1803 ----------------- Louisiana Purchase
1812-1815 ----------- War of 1812
                       Alamo
1846-48 -------------- Mexican War
                       California Gold Rush
                       Little Big Horn

People Places and Topics to Read About

George Washington	Thomas Jefferson
Alexander Hamilton	James Madison
John Adams	Andrew Jackson
Benjamin Banneker	John Charles Fremont
Robert Fulton	Buffalo Bill
Old Ironsides	Wild Bill Hickok
Battle of New Orleans	Sitting Bull
Sam Houston	Crazy Horse
The Alamo	General Armstrong Custer
Davey Crockett	Dorothea Dix
James Monroe	Sojourner Truth
Zachary Taylor	Cyrus McCormick
General Santa Anna	The stagecoach
Lewis & Clark	Oregon Trail
Trail of Tears	

Inventions and Innovations

Transcontinental Railroad	Telegraph
Cotton gin	Pony Express
Erie Canal	

Important Documents or Policies to Research

Federalism	Homestead Act of 1862
Monroe Doctrine	Manifest Destiny

Famous Phrases

"There's gold in them thar hills"	"Go west young man!"
"We have met the enemy and they are ours"	"Remember the Alamo!"

***Everything You Need to Know About American History Homework*:**

A Desk Reference for Students and Parents

"Westward Ho! The Expansion West"   **Pages 37-53**

UNIT 4: STUDY HELPS

Study Topics from E. D. Hirsch's _What Your 4th Grader Needs to Know_

Study Topics from E. D. Hirsch's _What Your 5th Grader Needs to Know_

Optional Activities

(Page numbers are keyed to _Everything You Need to Know About American History Homework_)

- Memorize the order of the presidents up to the Civil War (p. 124)
- On a map, label and date territories acquired during the Westward Expansion (p. 42)
- On a map, trace the route taken by Lewis and Clark to the Pacific (pp. 37-39)
- Pretend that you are a member of Lewis and Clark's Expedition and write a letter home explaining some of what you've experienced and seen
- On a map, trace the major overland routes of expansion (pp.40-41)
- Compose a telegraph message and write it out in Morse code
- On a map of the world, identify and label the locations of sea battles during the War of 1812

UNIT 4 READING LISTS

In-Print or Easily Found

- ☐ *The Pioneers Go West,* George Stewart
- ☐ *The California Gold Rush,* May McNeer we own
- ☐ *Custer's Last Stand,* Quentin Reynolds
- ☐ *Buffalo Bill,* Ingri and Edgar Parin D'Aulaire
- ☐ *Make Way for Sam Houston,* Jean Fritz
- ☐ *Buffalo Hunt,* Russell Freedman
- ☐ *Children of the Wild West,* Russell Freedman
- ☐ *Bold Journey,* Charles Bohner
- ☐ *Of Courage Undaunted,* James Daugherty
- ☐ *Davey Crockett: His Own Story: A Narrative of the Life of David Crockett of the State of Tennessee,* David Crockett

Landmarks (out-of-print)

- ☐ *Alexander Hamilton and Aaron Burr,* Anna Erskine and Russel Crouse
- ☐ *Thomas Jefferson, Father of Democracy,* Vincent Sheean
- ☐ *The Barbary Pirates,* C.S. Forester
- ☐ *Old Ironsides, the Fighting Constitution,* Harry Hansen
- ☐ *General Brock and Niagara Falls,* Samuel Hopkins Adams
- ☐ *The Louisiana Purchase,* Robert Tallant
- ☐ *Dolly Madison,* Jane Mayer
- ☐ *Robert Fulton and the Steamboat,* Ralph Nading Hill
- ☐ *The Pirate Lafitte and the Battle of New Orleans,* Robert Tallant
- ☐ *The Erie Canal,* Samuel Hopkins Adams
- ☐ *War Chief of the Seminoles,* May McNeer
- ☐ *Sam Houston, Tallest Texan,* William Johnson
- ☐ *John James Audubon,* Margaret and John Kieran
- ☐ *Clipper Ship Days,* John Jennings
- ☐ *Tippecanoe and Tyler, Too!,* Stanley Young
- ☐ *Commodore Perry and the Opening of Japan,* Ferdinand Kuhn
- ☐ *The World's Greatest Showman: The Life of P.T. Barnum,* J. Bryan III
- ☐ **Kit Carson and the Wild Frontier,* Ralph Moody
- ☐ *Sequoyah: Leader of the Cherokees,* Alice Marriott
- ☐ *Daniel Boone,* John Mason Brown
- ☐ *The Lewis and Clark Expedition,* Richard L. Neuberger
- ☐ *The Santa Fe Trail,* Samuel Hopkins Adams
- ☐ *Trappers and Traders of the Far West,* James Daugherty
- ☐ *Davy Crockett,* Stewart H. Holbrook
- ☐ *To California by Covered Wagon,* George R. Stewart
- ☐ *The Coming of the Mormons,* Jim Kjelgaard
- ☐ *The First Overland Mail,* Robert Pinkerton
- ☐ *The Pony Express,* Samuel Hopkins Adams
- ☐ *Buffalo Bill's Great Wild West Show,* Walter Havighurst
- ☐ *Wild Bill Hickok Tames the West,* Stewart H. Holbrook
- ☐ *The Building of the First Transcontinental Railroad,* Adele Gutman Nathan
- ☐ *Up the Trail from Texas,* J. Frank Dobie
- ☐ *The Texas Rangers,* Will Henry

- ☐ *The Story of San Francisco*, Charlotte Jackson
- ☐ *Remember the Alamo!*, Robert Penn Warren
- ☐ *Geronimo: Wolf of the Warpath*, Ralph Moody
- ☐ *Heroines of the Early West*, Nancy Wilson Ross
- ☐ *The Golden Age of Railroads*, Stewart H. Holbrook
- ☐ *The Story of Oklahoma*, Lon Tinkle

Other Out-of-Print Treasures

- ☐ *The Story of the War of 1812*, Colonel Red Reeder
- ☐ *The Story of the Mexican War*, Colonel Red Reeder
- ☐ *Westward Adventures: True Stories of 6 Pioneers*, William O. Steele
- ☐ *Riders of the Pony Express*, Ralph Moody (North Star)
- ☐ *Wells Fargo*, Ralph Moody (North Star)
- ☐ *Stagecoach West*, Ralph Moody
- ☐ *The Old Trails West*, Ralph Moody
- ☐ *The Battle of Lake Erie*, F. Van Wyck Mason (North Star)
- ☐ *The Battles for New Orleans*, F. Van Wyck Mason (North Star)
- ☐ *The First Steamboat on the Mississippi*, Sterling North
- ☐ *Robert Fulton, Boy Craftsman*, Marguerite Henry
- ☐ *Chief Joseph of the Nez Perces*, Shannon Garst
- ☐ *James Bowie and his Famous Knife*, Shannon Garst
- ☐ *Buffalo Bill,* Shannon Garst
- ☐ *Jim Bridger: Greatest of the Mountain Men*, Shannon Garst
- ☐ *Andrew Jackson, Frontier Statesman*, Clara Ingram Judson
- ☐ *Yankee Clippers, The Story of Donald McKay*, Clara Ingram Judson
- ☐ *Reaper Man, The Story of Cyrus McCormick*, Clara Ingram Judson
- ☐ *John Charles Fremont: The Last American Explorer*, Ronald Syme
- ☐ *Vancouver, Explorer of the Pacific Coast*, Ronald Syme
- ☐ *Andrew Jackson*, Margaret Coit
- ☐ *Buckskin Brigade*, Jim Kjelgaard
- ☐ *Sitting Bull, Champion of His People*, Shannon Garst
- ☐ *The Story of Andrew Jackson*, Enid LaMonte Meadowcroft

Advanced Reader or Read-Aloud

- ☐ *Cowboys, Indians and Gunfighters: The Story of the Cattle Kingdom*, Albert Marrin
- ☐ *1812: The War Nobody Won*, Albert Marrin
- ☐ *Plains Warrior: Chief Quanah Parker and the Comanches*, Albert Marrin
- ☐ **War Clouds in the West: Indians and Cavalrymen 1860-1890*, Albert Marrin
- ☐ *Empires Lost and Won: The Spanish Heritage in the Southwest*, Albert Marrin

* denotes family favorite

Historical Fiction

- ☐ *The Buffalo Knife*, William O. Steele
- ☐ *The Far Frontier*, William O. Steele
- ☐ **Caddie Woodlawn*, Carol Ryrie Brink, Newbery *we own*
- ☐ *By the Great Horn Spoon*, Sid Fleischman
- ☐ *Seabird, Holling Clancy Hollings* (life on board a whaling ship), (Newbery Honor)
- ☐ *Tree in the Trail*, Holling Clancy Hollings (Santa Fe Trail history)
- ☐ *All Sail Set, A Romance of the Flying Cloud*, Armstrong Sperry (Newbery Honor)
- ☐ *Winter Danger*, William O. Steele
- ☐ *Flaming Arrows*, William O. Steele
- ☐ *Wilderness Trail*, William O. Steele
- ☐ *Tomahawks and Trouble*, William O. Steele
- ☐ *Young Mac of Fort Vancouver*, Mary Jane Carr (Newbery Honor)
- ☐ *Prairie Songs*, Pam Conrad
- ☐ *Sarah, Plain and Tall*, Patricia MacLachlan (Newbery)
- ☐ *A Gathering of Days*, Joan Blos (Newbery)
- ☐ *On to Oregon*, Honore Morrow
- ☐ *By Wagon and Flatboat*, Enid Meadowcroft
- ☐ *Hitty, Her First Hundred Years*, Rachel Field (Newbery)
- ☐ *Little House books*, Laura Ingalls Wilder
- ☐ *Moccasin Trail*, Eloise Jarvis McGraw (Newbery Honor)
- ☐ *Old Yeller,* Fred Gipson (Newbery Honor)
- ☐ *Davy Crockett's Earthquake*, William O. Steele (tall tales)
- ☐ *Yankee Thunder: The Legendary Life of Davy Crockett*, Irwin Shapiro

**Poetry,
Prose
and Songs**

Songs

"The Star-Spangled Banner", Francis Scott Key
"Whoopee Ti Yi Yo, Git Along Little Dogies", John A. Lomax
"Home, Sweet Home", John Howard Payne
"America", Samuel F. Smith
"On Top of Old Smoky"
"O, Susanna", Stephen Foster
"The Erie Canal"
"Sweet Betsy from Pike"

Poetry

"John Adams", Rosemary and Stephen Vincent Benet
"Lewis and Clark", Rosemary and Stephen Vincent Benet
"Thomas Jefferson", Rosemary and Stephen Vincent Benet
"The Ballad of William Sycamore", Stephen Vincent Benet
"Old Ironsides", Oliver Wendell Holmes
"The Flower-Fed Buffaloes", Vachel Lindsay
"Song of the Settlers", Jessamyn West
"I Hear America Singing", Walt Whitman

Civil War and Reconstruction
(1861-1877)

**Dates
and Events
to Remember**

The Missouri Compromise
John Brown's assault on Harper's Ferry
1861-65--------------- The Civil War
Emancipation Proclamation
1865------------------- Lincoln assassinated
1865-1877------------ Reconstruction

**People
Places and Topics
to Read About**

Abraham Lincoln	Andrew Johnson
Jefferson Davis	Eli Whitney
Harriet Beecher Stowe	Jim Crow Laws
Harriet Tubman	Ku Klux Klan
Underground Railroad	Clara Barton
John Brown at Harper's Ferry	Sojourner Truth
Stonewall Jackson	Appomattox Courthouse
Fort Sumter	Bull Run
Gettysburg	March to The Sea
Vicksburg	Richmond
Ulysses S. Grant	54th Massachusetts Volunteer Regi-
Robert E. Lee	ment

**Inventions
and Innovations**

Monitor and the Merrimac
Cotton Gin

**Important
Documents
or Policies
to Research**

The Lincoln-Douglas Debates	Gettysburg Address
The Missouri Compromise	The Dred Scott Decision
The Emancipation Proclamation	Uncle Tom's Cabin

**Famous
Phrases**

"A house divided against itself cannot stand"
"a government of the people, by the people, for the people"

Everything You Need to Know About American History Homework:
A Desk Reference for Students and Parents

"A Nation Divided"
"The Civil War"

Pages 54-71

UNIT 5: STUDY HELPS

Study Topics from E. D. Hirsch's *What Your 5th Grader Needs to Know*

- North and South
- The Missouri Compromise
- *Uncle Tom's Cabin*
- How Some Slaves Resisted
- The Dred Scott Decision
- The Lincoln-Douglas Debates
- John Brown at Harper's Ferry
- The Argument over States' Rights
- Lincoln Elected: Southern States Secede
- Fort Sumter: The Civil War Begins
- Eager to Fight
- The Confederacy
- The Soldiers
- Robert E. Lee
- Ulysses S. Grant
- The Emancipation Proclamation
- African-American Troops in the Civil War
- A Brave Black Regiment
- The Misery of War
- Gettysburg: A Turning Point in the War
- Lincoln's Gettysburg Address
- Sherman's March to the Sea
- Richmond Falls
- Surrender at Appomattox
- Lincoln is Assassinated
- Reconstruction: Repairing the "House Divided"
- Johnson's Plan for Reconstruction
- Black Codes
- Scalawags and Carpetbaggers
- The Freedman's Bureau
- The Impeachment of President Johnson
- Three Important Amendments: Thirteenth, Fourteenth and Fifteenth
- The End of Reconstruction

Optional Activities

(Page numbers are keyed to *Everything You Need to Know About American History Homework*)

- On a map, label the slave and free states and territories at the time of the Missouri Compromise (p. 61)
- On a map, draw and label the Union and Confederate states (p. 61)
- Draw a person in Confederate uniform and one wearing a Union Army uniform
- Since railroads played a significant role in war for the first time, draw a map showing where the railroads were located

UNIT 5: READING LISTS

In-Print or Easily Found

- ☐ *Commander-in-Chief: Abraham Lincoln and the Civil War*, Albert Marrin
- ☐ *Virginia's General: Robert E. Lee and the Civil War*, Albert Marrin
- ☐ *Unconditional Surrender: U.S. Grant and the Civil War*, Albert Marrin
- ☐ *Abe Lincoln: Log Cabin to White House*, Sterling North (Landmark)
- ☐ *Gettysburg*, MacKinlay Kantor (Landmark) we own
- ☐ *Freedom Train*, Dorothy Sterling
- ☐ *Lincoln: A Photobiography*, Russell Freedman, Newbery
- ☐ *Stonewall*, Jean Fritz
- ☐ *Bull Run*, Paul Fleischmann
- ☐ *The Boys' War: Confederate and Union Soldiers Talk about the Civil War*, Edited by Jim Murphy
- ☐ *Abraham Lincoln*, Ingri and Edgar Parin D'Aulaire
- ☐ *Undying Glory: The Story of the Massachusetts 54th Regiment*, Clinton Cox
- ☐ *Clara Barton: Founder of the American Red Cross*, Susan Sloate
- ☐ *Behind Rebel Lines: The Incredible Story of Emma Edmonds, Civil War Spy*, Seymour Reit
- ☐ *Harriet Beecher Stowe and the Beecher Preachers*, Jean Fritz

Landmarks (out-of-print)

- ☐ *Lincoln and Douglas: The Years of Decision*, Regina Z. Kelly
- ☐ *Robert E. Lee and the Road of Honor*, Hodding Carter
- ☐ *The Monitor and the Merrimac*, Fletcher Pratt
- ☐ *Lee and Grant at Appomattox*, MacKinlay Kantor
- ☐ *Clara Barton, Founder of the American Red Cross*, Helen Dore Boylston
- ☐ *Stonewall Jackson*, Jonathan Daniels

Other Out-of-Print Treasures

- ☐ *The Story of the Civil War*, Colonel Red Reeder
- ☐ *Frederick Douglass: Voice of Freedom*, Eric Weiner
- ☐ *Anchors Aweigh: The Story of David Glasgow Farragut*, Jean Lee Latham
- ☐ *Robert E. Lee*, Jonathan Daniels (North Star)
- ☐ *The Northern Generals*, Colonel Red Reeder
- ☐ *The Southern Generals*, Colonel Red Reeder
- ☐ *Frederick Douglass: Slave, Fighter, Freeman*, Arna Bontemps
- ☐ *General Phil Sheridan and the Union Cavalry*, Milton Lomask

Historical Fiction

- ☐ *The Perilous Road*, William O. Steele (Newbery Honor)
- ☐ *Rifles for Watie*, Harold Keith (Newbery)
- ☐ *Shades of Gray*, Carolyn Reeder
- ☐ *Across Five Aprils*, Irene Hunt (Newbery Honor)
- ☐ *By Secret Railway*, Enid Meadowcroft
- ☐ *Brady*, Jean Fritz
- ☐ *Thee, Hannah*, Marguerite D'Angeli
- ☐ *Turn Homeward, Hannalee*, Patricia Beatty (some strong language)

**Poetry,
Prose
and Songs**

Prose

Excerpt from A Narrative of the Life of Frederick Douglass (Hirsh's Grade 4
Book)
Gettysburg Address

Poetry

"Barbara Frietchie", John Greenleaf Whittier
"O Captain! My Captain!", Walt Whitman
"Sheridan's Ride", Thomas Buchanan Read

Songs

"Go Down, Moses"
"Dixie", Daniel Decatur Emmett
"Battle Hymn of the Republic", Julia Ward Howe
"Swing Low, Sweet Chariot", Negro Spiritual

Industrial Revolution and the Rise of American World Leadership (1878-1918)

Dates and Events to Remember

1898-1900 ----------- Spanish-American War
Alaska Gold Rush
Wright brothers fly airplane at Kitty Hawk
1914-18 -------------- World War I
The Sinking of the Lusitania
1917 ----------------- America enters World War I

People Places and Topics to Read About

Andrew Carnegie
John D. Rockefeller
Henry Ford
Thomas Alva Edison
Alexander Graham Bell
George Washington Carver
J. P. Morgan
Statue of Liberty
Ellis Island
Alaskan Gold Rush
William Jennings Bryan
Jane Addams and Hull House
Booker T. Washington
W.E.B. Du Bois
Wilbur and Orville Wright

Theodore Roosevelt
Mark Twain
Nineteenth Amendment
San Juan Hill
Cuban War for Independence
Maine
San Francisco Earthquake
Woodrow Wilson
League of Nations
Helen Keller
Eddie Rickenbacker
Johnstown Flood
Susan B. Anthony
Treaty of Versailles
Russian Revolution

Inventions and Innovations to know

electricity
telephone
tank
labor unions

aviation
automobile
assembly line
submarine

Famous Phrases

"Walk softly and carry a big stick"
"How the other half lives"
"Remember the *Maine*!"
"Yellow journalism"

"The Bully pulpit"
"...your tired, your poor, your huddled masses yearning to breathe free"
"A war to end all wars"

Everything You Need to Know About American History Homework:
A Desk Reference for Students and Parents

"Industrialization"
"The 20th Century—America as World Leader"

Pages 72-90

UNIT 6: STUDY HELPS

- Industrialists, Capitalists and Monopolies
- Working in the Industrial Age
- More Immigrants Arrive in the Land of Opportunity
- Farmers and the Rise of Populism
- Jane Addams and Hull House
- Reform for African-Americans: Washington and Du Bois
- Women Struggle for Equal Rights
- Theodore Roosevelt: Trust-Buster and Conservationist
- The Cuban War for Independence and the Spanish-American War
- Cuba Fights for Independence
- "Yellow Journalism" urges Americas war involvement
- The United States becomes a world power

Study Topics from E. D. Hirsch's *What Your 5th Grader Needs to Know*

- World War I
- The deadliest war ever
- American neutrality
- The sinking of the *Lusitania*
- America enters the war
- Revolution comes to Russia
- The end of the war

Study Topics from E. D. Hirsch's *What Your 5th Grader Needs to Know*

Optional Activities
(Page numbers are keyed to *Everything You Need to Know About American History Homework*)

- Memorize the order of presidents from the Civil War through WWI (pp. 124-125)
- On a map of the Americas, demonstrate how much distance the Panama Canal saved on the trip between New York and San Francisco
- On a map of the Americas, show the territories gained by the U. S. in the Spanish-American War (p. 74)
- On a map of Europe, color code the countries and indicate which were members of the allies, and which were considered "Central Powers" (p. 74)

UNIT 6: READING LISTS

In-Print or Easily Found

- ☐ *The Yanks Are Coming: The United States in the First World War*, Albert Marrin
- ☐ *The Spanish-American War*, Albert Marrin
- ☐ *The Story of Thomas Alva Edison*, Margaret Cousins (Landmark)
- ☐ *The Wright Brothers: Pioneers of American Aviation*, Quentin Reynolds (Landmark)
- ☐ *Bully for You, Teddy Roosevelt*, Jean Fritz
- ☐ *Immigrant Kids*, Russell Freedman
- ☐ *Thomas Edison: The Great American Inventor*, Louise Egan
- ☐ *The Story of My Life*, Helen Keller
- ☐ *George Washington Carver*, Rackham Holt
- ☐ *The Wright Brothers: How They Invented the Airplane*, Russell Freedman (Newbery Honor)

Landmarks (out-of-print)

- ☐ *Mr. Bell Invents the Telephone*, Katherine B. Shippen
- ☐ *Teddy Roosevelt and the Rough Riders*, Henry Castor
- ☐ *The Panama Canal*, Bob Considine
- ☐ *The Doctors Who Conquered Yellow Fever*, Ralph Nading Hill
- ☐ *George Washington Carver: The Story of a Great American*, Anne Terry White
- ☐ *The Conquest of the North and South Poles*, Russell Owen
- ☐ *The Early Days of Automobiles*, Elizabeth Janeway
- ☐ *Wyatt Earp: U.S. Marshal*, Stewart H. Holbrook
- ☐ *General Pershing and World War I*, Henry Castor
- ☐ *Andrew Carnegie and the Age of Steel*, Katherine B. Shippen
- ☐ *The First Transatlantic Cable*, Adele Gutman Nathan
- ☐ *The Alaska Gold Rush*, May McNeer
- ☐ *Disaster at Johnstown: The Great Flood*, Hildegarde Dolson
- ☐ *Young Mark Twain and the Mississippi*, Harnett T. Kane
- ☐ *The Copper Kings of Montana*, Marian T. Place
- ☐ *Flying Aces of World War I*, Gene Gurney

Other Out-of-Print Treasures

- ☐ *Young Thomas Edison*, Sterling North (North Star)
- ☐ *Mark Twain and the River*, Sterling North (North Star)
- ☐ *The Story of the Spanish American War*, Colonel Red Reeder
- ☐ *The Story of the First World War*, Colonel Red Reeder
- ☐ *Mr. Justice Holmes*, Clara Ingram Judson (Newbery Honor)
- ☐ *Andrew Carnegie*, Clara Ingram Judson
- ☐ *Theodore Roosevelt: Fighting Patriot*, Clara Ingram Judson (Newbery Honor)

Historical Fiction

- ☐ *The Call of the Wild*, Jack London
- ☐ *Earthquake at Dawn*, Kristiana Gregory
- ☐ *Cheaper by the Dozen*, Frank Gilbreth, Jr. and Ernestine Gilbreth Carey
- ☐ *Little Women*, Louisa May Alcott
- ☐ *Understood Betsy*, Dorothy Canfield
- ☐ *Where the Red Fern Grows*, Wilson Rawls
- ☐ *Rebecca of Sunnybrook Farm*, Kate Douglas Wiggins
- ☐ *Five Little Peppers and How They Grew*, Margaret Sidney

Special: Autobiography

- ☐ *Fighting the Flying Circus*, Eddie Rickenbacker
  (out of print but available online at www.tntech.edu/www/acad/hist/gilprog.html)
- ☐ *Little Britches* series by Ralph Moody

Titles in order include:

- ☐ **Little Britches: Father and I Were Ranchers*
- ☐ **Man of the Family*
- ☐ **The Home Ranch*
- ☐ *Mary Emma and Company*
- ☐ *The Fields of Home*
- ☐ *Shaking the Nickel Bush*
- ☐ *The Dry Divide*
- ☐ *Horse of a Different Color: Reminiscenses of a Kansas Drover*

(The last three books chronicle Ralph's adventures as an adult)

Prose, Poetry and Song

The Pledge of Allegiance (first appeared in a magazine in 1892)
"The New Colossus", Emma Lazarus
"The Ballad of John Henry"
"Home on the Range"
"I've Been Working on the Railroad"
"Clementine"
"America the Beautiful", Katharine Lee Bates
"Take Me Out to the Ballgame", Albert von Tilzer and Jack Norworth

WWI Songs

"Over There", George M. Cohan
"Oh, How I Hate to Get Up in the Morning", Irving Berlin
"The Marine's Hymn"
"The Field Artillery Song" (caisson song), Edmund L. Gruber

Boom, Depression and WWII (1919-1945)

Dates and Events to Remember

1929 ------------------	Stock Market Crash/Depression begins
1939 ------------------	Hitler invades Poland (WWII begins)
Dec. 7, 1941 ---------	Japan attacks Pearl Harbor/U.S. enters war
June 6, 1944 -------------	D-Day: Normandy Invasion
	Germany surrenders/V-E Day
Aug. 6, 1945 ----------	U. S. drops nuclear bomb on Hiroshima
	Japan surrenders, WWII ends

People Places and Topics to Read About

Pre-WWII

Charles Lindbergh

Amelia Earhart

Charlie Chaplin

George Gershwin

Louis Armstrong

Prohibition

Franklin Delano Roosevelt

Herbert Hoover

Golden Gate Bridge

The Dust Bowl

Harlem Renaissance

World War II

Winston Churchill

Dwight D. Eisenhower

Benito Mussolini

Emperor Hirohito

Axis and Allied Powers

Charles de Gaulle

Douglas MacArthur

George S. Patton

Erwin Rommel

Adolf Hitler

Joseph Stalin

Bataan Death March

Okinawa

Guadalcanal

Iwo Jima

Japanese Internment Camps

Yalta

Harry S Truman

Holocaust

Midway

Inventions and Innovations to know

jet propulsion

television

quantum physics

nuclear power

Important Documents and Policies

National Labor Relations Act (1935)

Taft-Hartley Act (1947)

19th Amendment

Social Security Act

New Deal

Famous Expressions

"Lucky Lindy"

"A day that will live in infamy"

"The only thing we have to fear is fear itself"

"I shall return"

"American know-how"

"Fireside chat"

"A chicken in every pot"

Everything You Need to Know About American History Homework:

A Desk Reference for Students and Parents

"Industrialization"

"The 20th Century—America as World Leader"

Pages 91-107

UNIT 7: STUDY HELPS

Study
Topics
from E. D. Hirsch's
*What Your 6th
Grader Needs to
Know*

- America Turns Inward
- Prosperity and Progress
- New Forms of Entertainment
- The Roaring Twenties
- African-Americans Move North
- The Harlem Renaissance
- The Great Depression
- Herbert Hoover
- The New Deal
- Social Security
- The "Indian New Deal"
- The Dust Bowl and the "Okies"
- Hitler's Rise to Power in Germany
- World War II Begins
- Should America Fight?
- Pearl Harbor Pushes America to War
- The Axis Versus the Allies
- The Division of Poland
- The Axis at High Tide
- The Holocaust
- The War in Europe and Africa
- The War in the Pacific
- The Home Front
- Internment of Japanese-Americans
- D-Day
- Meeting at Yalta
- FDR Dies; Truman Becomes President
- Victory in Europe
- The Atomic Bomb
- Hiroshima, Nagasaki & Surrender of Japan

Optional Activities
(Page numbers are keyed to *Everything You Need to Know About American History Homework*)

- On a map of Europe, use different colors to identify Allied and Axis nations (p. 98)
- On a map of the Pacific Ocean, find the islands of famous battles, such as Midway, Wake Island, Iwo Jima, Okinawa, and Attu & Kiska (in the Aleutians)
- On a map of Europe, identify the location of battlefields, such as Dunkirk, Anzio, the D-Day Landings, and Bastogne
- Imagine you are trying to support a family during the depression. Write a piece describing what your day might be like (p. 95)

**In Print
or Easily Found**

☐ *The Spirit of St. Louis*, Charles Lindbergh
☐ *Amelia Earhart: Pioneer of the Sky*, John Parlin

World War II
☐ *Overlord: D-Day and the Invasion of Europe*, Albert Marrin
☐ *Victory in the Pacific*, Albert Marrin
☐ *Airman's War*, Albert Marrin
☐ *The Secret Armies: Spies, Counterspies and Saboteurs in World War II*, Albert Marrin
☐ *Stalin: Russia's Man of Steel*, Albert Marrin (mature subject matter)
☐ *Hitler*, Albert Marrin (mature subject matter)
☐ *The Story of D-Day: June 6, 1944*, Bruce Bliven, Jr. (Landmark)
☐ *Air Raid—Pearl Harbor!*, Theodore Taylor
☐ *The Hiding Place*, Corrie Ten Boom (mature subject matter)
☐ *The Story of the Trapp Family Singers*, Maria Augusta Trapp

**Landmarks
(out of print)**

☐ *Thirty Seconds Over Tokyo*, Ted Lawson and Bob Considine
☐ *Guadalcanal Diary*, Richard Tregaskis
☐ *The Story of the Paratroops*, George Weller
☐ *Battle for the Atlantic*, Jay Williams
☐ *From Pearl Harbor to Okinawa*, Bruce Bliven, Jr.
☐ *Great American Fighter Pilots of World War II*, Robert Loomis
☐ *John F. Kennedy and PT-109*, Richard Tregaskis
☐ *The Seabees of World War II*, Commander Edmund L. Castillo
☐ *The Flying Tigers*, John Toland
☐ *The U.S. Frogman of World War II*, Wyatt Blassingame
☐ *From Casablanca to Berlin*, Bruce Bliven, Jr.
☐ *The Battle of the Bulge*, John Toland
☐ *The Battle for Iwo Jima*, John Toland
☐ *Combat Nurses of World War II*, Wyatt Blassingame
☐ *The Battle of Britain*, Quentin Reynolds
☐ *The Rise and Fall of Adolf Hitler*, William L. Shirer
☐ *The Sinking of the Bismarck*, William L. Shirer
☐ *The Commandos of World War II*, Hodding Carter
☐ *Dwight D. Eisenhower*, Malcolm Moos
☐ *Midway: Battle for the Pacific*,
☐ *Medical Corps Heroes of World War II*
☐ *Winston Churchill*, Quentin Reynolds
☐ *The Story of Atomic Energy*, Laura Fermi

**Other
Out of Print
Treasures**

☐ *The Story of World War II, Vols. I and II*, Colonel Red Reeder
☐ *The Complete Life of Winston Churchill*, Leonard Wibberley

**Historical
Fiction**

☐ *Blue Willow*, Doris Gates (Newbery Honor)
☐ *Ida Early Comes Over the Mountain*, Robert Burch
☐ *Roll of Thunder, Hear My Cry*, Mildred Taylor (Newbery)
☐ *Sounder*, William Armstrong (Newbery)
☐ *The Yearling*, Marjorie K. Rawlings
☐ *Strawberry Girl*, Lois Lenski (Newbery)

Word War II Historical Fiction

☐ *Twenty and Ten*, Claire Huchet Bishop
☐ *Snow Treasure*, Marie McSwigan
☐ *The Winged Watchman*, Hilda von Stockum
☐ *The Mitchells: Five for Victory*, Hilda von Stockum
☐ *The Borrowed House*, Hilda von Stockum
☐ *Escape from Warsaw*, Ian Serraillier
☐ *When Hitler Stole Pink Rabbit*, Judith Kerr
☐ *Number the Stars*, Lois Lowry, (Newbery)
☐ *Journey to America*, Sonia Levitin
☐ *Miracles on Maple Hill*, Virginia Sorensen, (Newbery)
☐ *When Jays Fly to Barbmo*, Margaret Balderson
☐ *The Ark*, Margot Benary-Isbert
☐ *Rowan Farm*, Margot Benary-Isbert
☐ *Dangerous Spring*, Margot Benary-Isbert
☐ *Silence over Dunkerque*, John R. Tunis
☐ *Journey to Topaz*, Yoshiko Uchido
☐ *The Dolphin Crossing*, Jill Paton Walsh
☐ *The House of Sixty Fathers,* Meindert de Jong, (Newbery Honor)
☐ *Carrie's War*, Nina Bawden
☐ *North of Danger*, Dale Fife
☐ *When the Sirens Wailed*, Noel Streatfield

WWII Adventure Stories by Robb White:

Flight Deck
The Frogmen
Surrender
Torpedo Run
Up Periscope
The Survivor

Songs

"Happy Days Are Here Again", Milton Ager and Jack Yellen
"Brother, Can You Spare a Dime"? E.Y. Harburg and Jay Gorney
"God Bless America", Irving Berlin
"This is the Army, Mr. Jones", Irving Berlin
"This Land is Your Land", Woody Guthrie
"Anchors Aweigh", Charles A. Zimmerman
"The Army Air Cops", Robert Crawford

* family favorite

**Prose,
Poetry
and Song**

The American Century
(1946-present)

Dates and Events to Remember

Beginning of the Cold War/nuclear arms race
1950-53 ------ Korean War
Escalation of Vietnam War
President John F. Kennedy assassinated
March on Washington
Martin Luther King, Jr. and Robert Kennedy assassinated
American astronauts land on the moon
1963-1975 ---- Vietnam War
1973 --------- Supreme Court decides *Roe v. Wade*
1974 --------- Nixon Resigns
1991 --------- Collapse of Soviet Union/End of Cold War

People Places and Topics to Read About

Richard Nixon	Kent State Riot
Ronald Reagan	John Glenn
Harry S Truman	Neil Armstrong
Iron Curtain	Lyndon Johnson
Joseph McCarthy	Great Society
"Jim Crow" Laws	Malcolm X
Jackie Robinson	George Bush
Rosa Parks	Sputnik
Alan Shepherd	Cuban Missile Crisis
John F. Kennedy	Berlin Wall
Martin Luther King, Jr.	Watergate

Inventions and Innovations to know

penicillin	space flight
polio vaccine	computers
television	microwave technology
missile technology	

Important Documents and Policies

The Marshall Plan	The Civil Rights Act of 1964
Brown v. Board of Education	*Roe v. Wade*

Famous Expressions

"Give 'em Hell, Harry"
"Old soldiers never die, they simply fade away"
"Tune in, turn on, drop out"
"I have a dream"

"the back of the bus"
"That's one small step for man, one giant leap for mankind"
"Mr. Gorbachev, tear down this wall!"

Everything You Need to Know About American History Homework:
A Desk Reference for Students and Parents

"Events Since World War II"

Pages 110-112

UNIT 8: STUDY HELPS

To better understand the conflict between Communism and Capitalism, we also recommend reading in the World Civilization section "The Idea of Laissez Faire" and "Capitalism and Socialism."

Study Topics from E. D. Hirsch's *What Your 6th Grader Needs to Know*

The "Superpowers" Square Off
The Truman Doctrine and the Marshall Plan
The Cold War
The "Military-Industrial Complex" and the Nuclear Arms Race
McCarthyism
The Korean War Begins
Korea: Heroism and Frustration
American Life in the 1950's
A Decade of Prosperity
In the Suburbs and on the Road
The TV Age Begins
Segregation and Civil Rights
The "Jim Crow" Laws
A Philip Randolph: Pioneer for Civil Rights
African-Americans in the Armed Forces
Brown v. Board of Education
Rosa Parks and the Montgomery Bus Boycott
Martin Luther King, Jr.
King in Birmingham
The March on Washington

The Turbulent Sixties and After
John F. Kennedy
The Berlin Wall
The Cuban Missile Crisis
The Space Race
The Assassination of Kennedy
Lyndon Johnson and the Great Society
Johnson and Civil Rights
Malcolm X
The Civil Rights Movement Loses a Leader
Cesar Chavez Organizes Migrant Workers
Native Americans: From Termination to Self-Determination
The War in Vietnam
The War at Home: Hawks and Doves
The Youth Rebellion
The Vietnam War Ends
Watergate and the Fall of Richard Nixon
The Women's Liberation Movement
The Fight for the ERA
A Birthday Party

Optional Activities
(Page numbers are keyed to *Everything You Need to Know About American History Homework*)

- Memorize the order of presidents from Woodrow Wilson to the present (see p. 125)
- Create a timeline showing when various items were introduced, such as radio, television, the microwave, penicillin, the personal computer and the Internet
- On a map of Europe, color the countries that were ruled by communists during the Cold War

UNIT 8: READING LIST

In-Print or Easily Found

- ☐ **Teammates*, Peter Golenbock
- ☐ *Martin Luther King, Jr.: Dreams for a Nation*, Louise Quayle
- ☐ *Stalin: Russia's Man of Steel*, Albert Marrin (mature subject matter)
- ☐ *America and Vietnam: The Elephant and the Tiger*, Albert Marrin (mature subject matter)
- ☐ *Rachel Carson: Who Loved the Sea*, Jean Lee Latham
- ☐ *Profiles in Courage*, John F. Kennedy
- ☐ *The Rest of the Story*, Paul Harvey

Landmarks (out-of-print)

- ☐ *The War in Korea: 1950-53*, Robert Leckie
- ☐ *Hawaii: Gem of the Pacific*, Oscar Lewis
- ☐ *Americans into Orbit: The Story of Project Mercury*, Gene Gurney
- ☐ *Walk in Space: The Story of Project Gemini*,

Miscellaneous Landmarks

- ☐ *The Story of the U.S. Marines*, George Hunt
- ☐ *The F.B.I.*, Quentin Reynolds
- ☐ *The West Point Story*, Colonel Red Reeder
- ☐ *The Story of the Secret Service*, Ferdinand Kuhn
- ☐ *The Story of the Naval Academy*, Felix Riesenberg, Jr.
- ☐ *The Story of the U.S. Air Force*, Robert Loomis
- ☐ *The Story of the U.S. Coast Guard*, Eugene Rachlis
- ☐ *The Story of Submarines*, George Weller
- ☐ *The U. S. Border Patrol*, Clement Hellyer
- ☐ *Women of Courage*, Dorothy Nathan
- ☐ *Medal of Honor Heroes*, Colonel Red Reeder

Prose, Poetry and Song

Prose
- ☐ Inaugural Address of John F. Kennedy (Excerpted in Hirsch: pp. 30-32)
- ☐ "I Have a Dream", Martin Luther King (Excerpted in Hirsch: pp. 32-34)

HOW TO FIND OUT-OF-PRINT BOOKS

Finding out-of-print books is not as hard as you might think but it will require some extra effort on your part. Listed below are some places to visit in your search. Of course, you will never find all the books on these lists—but remember you don't have to either. You can easily find enough to keep your young reader busy for the course of the unit.

#1 Check Your Local Library

Plan to spend a morning (or afternoon) at your local library this summer. Any decent children's library will have a collection of Landmarks to start with. Search the library's computer for titles and particular authors and note on your guide which ones are available. Some books may be at other branches but it is a simple matter to have them sent to the branch nearest you when you need them. If there is a particular title you simply must find, try inter-library loan. This service will search the inventories of libraries outside your area for the book in question. Of course, a fee is usually charged for this service.

#2 Go to Library Book Sales

Every library periodically holds a book sale where they sell donations, slightly damaged books, extra copies of old bestsellers and books that are not circulating well. Many gems can often be found among the library's discards, but you have to get there early. Children's books are always the most popular and are picked over quickly. Often the first night of the sale is designated "Friends Night" and is open to members of the local Friends of the Library Association. Join and go the first night. It is well worth the membership fee.

Libraries sometimes have smaller sales throughout the year or sometimes a library will have a particular room or shelf set aside for discards throughout the year. Ask your local librarian.

#3 Check Thrift Stores

The Good Will and Salvation Army have one or more stores in almost every town with a population of over 10,000. Paperbacks typically run 25-50 cents and hardbacks 50 cents to two dollars. Some of the best bargains can be found here.

#4 Check Used Book Stores

One of my family's favorite outings is shopping at the local used bookstores. Not all used bookstores carry children's books so check first. We bought someone's collection of 20 plus Landmarks at a used bookstore once. Be forewarned—the books are sometimes pricey. Many of the books on our list are becoming collectors' items and used booksellers know this and charge accordingly.

#5 Search the Internet

If a book continues to elude you, try the Internet. BookFinder at www.bookfinder.com is a search engine that searches not only Amazon, but ABE, Interloc and many other used and new book sources. ABE Booksellers Online at www.abebooks.com is a single searchable database of hundreds of used booksellers worldwide. However, our family's personal Internet site is powells.com. Powell's is an enormous used book outlet in Oregon. Their selection is fantastic and you can make your purchases through a secure server similar to Amazon.